POETRY *of the*

PHOTOGRAPHS BY IAN BROWN

MOUNTAINS

MARK O'CONNOR

A MEGALONG BOOK

Contents

The Poetry of the Sandstone Mountains

We come to these mountains for special feelings that we might as well call poetry. And, at least in theory, the poetry of the mountains might be caught in words and presented on a page.

When there is an argument about preserving this region, it sometimes seems as if the only people who have words for their feelings are the greedy ones. Developers who want to make a "killing" will have all the dollar-and-cents arguments at the ready. But, in the face of approaching bulldozer treads, those of us who love the mountains may seem tongue-tied, as if what we felt was a mere dream or "airy nothing".

Precisely because these feelings come from the depths of our human nature, it is hard to trap them in words. How often instead we are reduced to a wordless expression of wonder, to buying a postcard or taking a second-rate snapshot!

What might a professional poet find to say about the mountains if he were given the chance to spend several months living in and with them?

In 1984 and 1985 the NSW National Parks Service decided to find out. As part of an innovative scheme known as the Park Writers Fellowship, they arranged for me to leave my home in North Queensland and live for some months in the sandstone mountains which encircle Sydney — the same rugged collar of mountains that once threatened to strangle the infant colony.

The result was over a hundred poems, designed as much to be heard as to be seen on a page. The better ones are presented here, together with superb colour photographs by Ian Brown, a ranger and photographer who has had the advantage of knowing remote areas of the Blue Mountains intimately.

What have Ian Brown and I found in the mountains? I might answer: "detail". A person's response to nature may be deep and intangible, but there is no single "nature feeling" — only hundreds of different feelings about different places and times. As Ian's photos suggest, every tree and cliff in these fantastically-weathered sandstone mountains is the only one of its kind, and evokes unique feelings.

We have also explored the human history of the mountains: from the convict cells of Hartley to the famous pioneers' dance-floor in the cave at Kanangra, and the ill-fated shale-oil mines of Newnes.

It can be a mistake for a poet to put names on his feelings, just as it might be for a photographer to try to photograph a feeling. I have usually preferred to convey an emotion indirectly, by re-creating (sometimes with precise scientific details) the scene which produced it. But I believe there are also times when it is more important to stop, after words have done what words can, and leave the reader's mind free.

This book starts where one might expect — with the broad panoramas and misty grandeurs. But its photos and poems soon move towards finer and finer focus; fine enough to visualise in "Love in the Blue Mountains" the precise fringe of hairs and petals by which a flower accepts or rejects a pollinating insect, and to suggest some similarities with human love. In fact the book celebrates a form of love — the detailed love that values and clings to the peculiarities of its environment, seeking neither to veil nor distort nor prettify them.

As human beings, we need the city too. But I suspect that only a book which looks in such detail at these delicate, spiky, particular places can suggest the many ways in which we also need and belong to the mountains and the natural world.

Mark O'Connor, 1988

Entering the National Park

There is too much of it,
too much like the rest of Australia.
You stop here not because here seems special
but because no place is real inside a car.
Overhead the wind keeps its bluster.
Clouds lighten and darken,
a play of inconstant air on stone.
From the road-verge the grass is a monotone
sprinkled with pale lemon wattles.
You enter it simply to get in, to begin, to make a move,
to shake from your skull the wasps of the city.
Once in, the risk of snakes, the twist
of a tussock under heel
will make the place real....

And, yes, straightaway you find
a crushed path through the tussocks — a wallaby road.
And you know that to hunters once
this would be the day's one thought and story.
But you cannot focus — your attention is global.
Crushed grass has no meaning on Tokyo's computers.
You do not need wallaby meat, or anything
from this strange place you are in.
You could walk on a snake
with your mind on another continent.

You find a wide space of flattened grass
— some communal hiding place —
and it starts to possess you.
You notice ants holding caucus around a dead bee,
or think how the trunks' worn stringy-bark
is like fur on the leather rug
where a cow has died in a paddock.
You are delicately distracted here,
by last night's phonecalls
and the first slight pull of hunger.
But for now you are in this place and of it
and all its million years
that will not last another decade.
You go back to the car, push a knob, turn a key,
and the dream land slides away.

Mist

Wading through mists of the mountains' breath
the wet white air,
once thought to be spirits of the dead,
and adding our quota.... This chill
that pulls neat water from the air
— a touched leaf trickles,
rolls tears along the blade.

Then the brief downpour.
Gullies, like washing machines switched on,
churn soil downhill.
The bush path is a tunnel into mist,
where every spider's web is seen
flagged out with silver buoys.
The lorikeet shuffles dejected feathers,
sipping weak nectar. A huntsman
crosses the path, half crushed
beneath the rain's broom;
it walks on grass stalks,
a blind tightrope walker
feeling in eight directions.
Hairs on a banksia leaf
repel drops and store the dryness
(tomorrow there may be fire).

In a Cloud

For three days we have lived inside a cloud,
watching a fog squeeze itself into droplets.
Sometimes it lowered and lifted around us,
white heights and dull grey
and once wispy white-blue.
Myrtle bushes were wet feather-dusters
that soaked us at the touch. The third day
from the high white country with no shadows,
descending the cliff I walked down into cloud
where by torchlight the trees were green-black.

The stream spilled water from a flute-edged rim,
once its bank, down half a hill.
Star-flowers in the never-rained overhangs
pulled water from the yielding air.
The heath's bell-sprays hung heavily
till an extra drop made an avalanche
that landing, cleared the branch below.
Young currawongs whined hard for grubs
their parents couldn't find.
Pointless. I turned upward
through the white safety-net of the fog.
That afternoon on slippery rungs I climbed
back a thousand feet to a whiter shade of fog,
listening to eagles calling through the white,
and the grounded crows complaining from the heights, waiting
for the vast air-ship to move on, trailing broad wisps,
from our steep, etched valley.

Govett's Leap Pass

The rock so sheer and high and mossed
seems a tundra turned on end,
a ribbon of silver water
blowing forever across its flank.

A blue-canvas of sky. You flinch
as a cloud pours over its top
like a swarm of white butterflies
— soon lost in slow-moving blue.

A river falls out of dry cliffs.
From vertical clefts
frogs chirp in their aerosol world
of glinting rain. The falls are white
dollops of downward mass;
they shimmer like fish-scales
in hot sun and breeze
— their gauze rainbows drift away.

Round the pool ferns grow
to the height spray can feed;
the drops landing forever,
on delicate moss.
Just once, for an hour
wind forced them away.
Result: black, and muddy.

Hanging Swamp

The swamp hangs from its vertical cliff,
a thin bulge of seepage in peat:
under the one-drop falls
the water-striders glide on sloping lakes
a hand's breadth wide, a hair's breadth deep,
the sundews' red rosettes ingest the midge
whose larvae swim in recurrent drops
that bottleneck, divide
like amoebae, dropping progeny.

Fluid that paramecium and blood-worm have used
enters and leaves as purely
as from the sky; comes out
softer than rainwater,
drips into spread-sheets, gathers
to trickles and spurts that fall,
half mist themselves on a thousand feet of air

— loose drops make a progress down-slope, skidding
and sheeting, with triumphal meetings
and ski-swift partings, to join at a later pass.
A ledge where the lake built a stiffer
layer of ooze one year is their ski-shoot.
Up from below comes an egg-shell crackle,
the hard drops breaking on rock

— to re-assemble for a final brink
among fern-forests, islands of tight-held mud,
vertical catchments for fingerling streams.
The hanging swamp feeds the waterfall
all the dry summer, an emblem of grace,
careless of the heights and depths of the world.

The Mountains

The peaks have many ways
to rise between or alongside others,
and in different light or weather.
We are all, they remind us, under the weather.

Round a bend, you surprise hunks of rock and cliff
jostling and manoeuvring, battleships in a bay.
Only parallax: but how swiftly those hillsides glide
as you hike, to a new formation, butting across
in each other's wake, finding gaps
in a squadron of lesser hills
where the main peak slices through,
leaving you somewhere precise, and precisely lost.

Monoliths

The fey high lonely rocks
stand in the Valley of Idols,
undercut by strata of soft coal.
The wind has no power till one day they topple,
unstacking sideways at the seams. (As yet,
the bee brings honey from the rim).
No human weight can hasten what
at the last will take six seconds —
cathedrals fall no faster than a pebble —
then sift to soil beneath a forest.

The wind's chisel gives them age,
incising blank foreheads. Behind,
as cleavage-planes etch patterns in the plateau,
their offspring stir and shape for later worlds.

Sandstone Mountains

Explorers making beelines for conspicuous mounts
were like river-boats trying to sail by compass.

The others, slipping from eel-swamp
to wallaby plateau, or down some snaking cleft,
knew the footholds.
Cliff-rim and creek-bed each rustled
with a different chance of meat.
In that up-land of cliffs and heather,
its light piercing like a crow's beak,
all the crooked paths went straight,
the compass-lines meandered.
They could scale the peaks, feast,
and be down by dusk, lying warm
and naked between two fires.

The shape of their valley
(some wrinkle in Earth's skin)
round a catfish lagoon where the two creeks met,
was the shape of a universe.
Ancestor-heroes spoke its dialect,
ate its regional cuisine.

Their Dreaming sites were sure and utter
— a bare half-dozen to a world.

Pagoda Country

Afloat on valley mists
we ride our drifting raft of rock,
like fleas on a cubist skull.
The rock's strata erode like stacked plates,
with rounded tops, or grey, scalloped cisterns
— an erratic pagoda, somehow blunt and disappointing
as the tops of mountains often are;
the highest peak a mere jut
thrust out obliquely
reaching anywhere but up,
one of earth's lumpy hobgoblin children,
squeezed out and abandoned,
broken with boils and eruptions,
a half-home to small furry parasites,
and prey to ceaseless sun and air.

The peaks scowl at each other
— a series of gnarled disasters.
The persistence of rivers
finds a way through.

And the wind howls "Resist like Prometheus —
I will grind your shank-bones into sand."

Hartley Courthouse

In the constables' room
black kettles and muffin-toasters,
a vast fire and powder horns
to frighten the shuffling felon.

The magistrate's private room is silent
with smell of oiled cedar.
Dieu et mon droit.
Nine tails of the whip.

A Greek temple built round a lock-up.
None in that court pleaded cold or hunger
to mitigate.

Bay windows behind the sentencer prove
that justice is beauty.

Everything about Hartley, 1839.

Establishment confirmed:
One Police Magistrate — £250 per annum.
One Chief Constable — £75 per annum.
One Watchhouse Keeper — three shillings per day.
One Ordinary Constable — two and ninepence per day.
Two Ordinary Constables — two and threepence per day.
One Scourger — two and six per day.

Blanket

Issued to Hartley native tribe, May 1841:
fifty blankets. Found to be insufficient.
Eighty blankets in 1842.
1846: twelve. "The Aborigines
of our district," a pioneer wrote,
"were always remarkably quiet,
and died out rapidly."

The Dance Floor in the Cave — Kanangra Walls

Folk came riding from two days round,
breakfast at the cousins', then "Off to the dance!"
Trotting up by the Thurat spires,
a last boulder-turn on the stock-path and
Hooley Dooley! — a cave
with a smooth plank floor, a fiddler and lanterns.
"Partners please..." for the genealogy waltz.

The rocks full of shell, like an ancient sea
moved lights in the ladies' eyes;
and the rhythmic moon of the violin,
glancing yellow in the overhang
made the finest sounds ever. And there was water,
sinking through sixty foot of sandstone
to plop in a barrel.
They danced till a pale light came up
through the tree-tops below. And after,
on coffee or whisky they rode home sleepless, to milking.
No one stole that plank-floor.

Dancing was serious business
— it could leave you courting
four days' ride away. And those eddying seas
would be life-time tides,
discussed and fathered and aunted over
before any step beyond this floor — and though its wood
is charcoal in some camper's fire,
many a stout old trunk survives in nursing homes
known to a score of grandchildren.

Newnes

— mushroomed and died in twenty years,
the mine blown up as if in spite,
the fire-towers wavering down to brick-piles
laced with blackberry, while rust-frayed
cables snake through the burnt-out scrub.

This is the engineer's nightmare: when
nature stirs in the night and rolls on his work.
Tadpoles will swarm in his settling tanks,
the long-legged huntsman breed in his coking kilns,
couples lay underfelt on his smelting floor,
lyrical abstractionists take for pure art
his beaten copper.

So much steel rides
on this scree's stopped avalanche.
And all was brought here
by the gentle tug of Uncle Bill's
and Grandma Johnson's wish
to have paraffin candles, a fridge,
and sixpenny kero tins
from the corner grocer.
The love of light
sliced tunnels through the plateau's seams,
where men crouched sixty hours a week
to scrape black paraffin
for an upper world of ice-cream,
cars and holidays.

The Hot Ridge

The hot ridge is snake country, eucalypt scented,
slither-and-scramble-land, smelling of honey and dust,
where no hot blood is needed.
The shrubs have minute fangs, needle-leaves that sting
like flagellants. The grevillea
is rosemary-leaved with unseen spines.

The thin soil's creeping ligno-tubers
are the heath's survival kit, what the membership
put aside for fire. The rocks
are nuggets of unopened soil.

The fire comes often.
Tracks, first made by bare black feet,
go straight with never a bush to block them.

This is bare clay and blow-fly country,
ant-hill and grass-tree land,
where the fierce black Formic Police
swarm in the trees, are unassailable on ground.
And the black snake winding in the heat
seems spawned by contrast from the midday sun,
a shadow slipping sideways like
a dark rod in God's yellow eye.

Fire-Stick Farming

To grow flowers in Blackheath, Australia,
set fire to your field. Let flame
singe the delicate dust-seeds
of native shrubs. Soon they sprout,
a thin patchwork of tufts, nameless and mixed,
on ground bare as if hoed.
Bright petals follow, as if you'd scattered
fifty packets of English seed; but not one
has a name Shakespeare knew: scarlet waratah
crowning its upright stake, flannel flower,
a grevillea in honey-and-orange
with juniper-mimicking leaves,
three nameless bulbs in cardinal shades,
and a heath whose giant blooms
seem threaded on grey wires.

The yellow dillwynia conjures blue moths that endure
their deaths from pale-lemon flower-spiders
whose grape bellies swell with eggs
to feed the thread-leg spider-wasp.
A huntsman in the open disdains escape,
dodging, faster than eye-blink, each lurch
of the sting — a game of hare and hound
among plants like moss with snowdrop flowers
and just a wisp of snake-slither.
In the hot calm the bees are loud,
working wings and elbows with an angry sound,
as you leap the tussocks, amazed
at your ignorant creation,
the shapes and passions hidden
in a sheet of flame.
And among them all
a new forest rising.

Love in the Blue Mountains

On this desert rock are herbs as faint and glaucous
as a ghost's shadow at noon,
pale grey-wire plants like bird-cotton
that take the minimum of light and heat.
In Spring they surprise with giant petals,
pouring honey, like rock oil, down the blazing slope.
The heath copulates through well-paid go-betweens
in a recondite fecundite pollination by proxy;
insects are its spiro-flagellants, bees its hairy gametes
in this land of the pollen-scented cloud
where a wind full of dry-blown plasm twirls
the ancient oceans caged in a spore of dust. Inside
swims the ancestral glob, a moist raft of chromosome rods.

From twig to conspecific twig, small gauzy helicopters ply,
airlifting protoplasm from severed worlds.
Each, fixed on two colours only,
navigates the vast Sargassum of grey,
touting its patent insemination kit
with proprietary borers and probes. *Clitoria* blossoms
flash vulvic petals, marvels of evolution,
that link pea-flower and mammal.
Visitors must be lured to the right place,
got to crawl over the stamens. (The hover-fly flits away,
a bright splash of pollen on his shoulder).
Mad bushmen have sworn that flowers converse in blank verse,
and bees buzz like Elizabethan groundlings:
"Pray sleep with my pale-petalled sister for me."
"Hairy fellow — this packet to my loved one.
It shall make honey for you."
"Look, pistils, a present from Romeo! Go see this fellow lodged."

In a world of twittering, twitching, vibrating sounds
I hear the sharp whine of a carpenter bee

tongue-in-grooving her way through a hakea bud.
Clouds of heath-flower float in a honeyed mist.
Here tongues are keys,
sprout flanges, ticklers, cotters, tappets —
not all pollen-tubes will open to all tongues
in Nature's get-what-you-can-reach bazaar.
The gum's broad florets are a smorgasbord laid
for all comers. Beetles plough them like furry tractors.
The lorikeet mates with his rainbow image in an eriostemon,
his brush tongue sweeping up seminal dust,
the sanctified bee-bread and nectar.
His spouse gobbles ant-infested flowers,
honeyed bells with a formic aftertaste
like a native *amaro*, honey and bitters.

And that pale spider's there,
who mimics the pistils of leptospermum.
His serrated legs draw visitors in
to a bloodier nectar, the slow chewing-off of heads
that still buzz with antennae in search of a treasure
desperately wanted for next Spring's eggs.
The wattle-bird drives a stiff raping brush,
that plucks out spider, pollen, nectar. A painted lady's
coil-tongue tickle-slips into a rutaceae bud,
while the red parrot's tongue-kiss on the red grevillea
lasts an ecstatic three seconds;
and the bulge goes down his throat, ruffling small orange feathers
in this place of reds and orange, of day flowers, bird colours.

But you need infra and ultra colours, long reds and short blues,
to pull in those extra-terrestrial hook-winged virgins,
those mutant furry spheroid wasps, the load-bearing bees;
ghost-white and luminous yellow are lures
for the powdery evening moths
that rustle like soft determined ladies;

and dark black is the honey flow,
dark as ti-tree creeks, and treacly as billy tea.

Ten tongue-lengths can feed in a handkerchief patch — a mosaic
of bird-flower, bee-flower, beetle-, fly-, moth- and bat-;
and *Banksia ericifolia* whose nectar icicles
are gnawed on dry August nights by marsupial mice;
though some think it nicer to mimic the smell of green meat
or the female parts of a disembodied wasp.

Orchids, fussy maters, insist on the right dab of pollen
from the right joint of the right insect,
protecting themselves with grilles and flaps
against petal-crashers and the great unwashed.
Some trap a travelling salesman, the pollen-bagged bee,
and won't let him go till the morning after. Some box
two or three, buzzing round in a cloud of orgiastic dust.
This one shoots its bundle — a skein of elastic threads,
and, stuck to a wasp, the pollinia flies through summer heat
to be reclaimed by precise adhesives.
Others shoot darts, half drown, tie up, and tease
the vibrating salesmen, or mad them with perfume.
The payoff? — two bundles of pollen precisely placed
for the next mock female.
The greenhood's labellum is itchy,
no floral skirt but a spring loaded flange
that slams a poor gnat against the stigma.
Bushflies hooked by the Leek Orchid's pheromone
walk down the spider's throat. And a tiny possum,
long-nosed, probes the banksia's muff.

Storm

The blow is coming! is coming now,
the pine-tops shriek and plunge.
Below no leaf is stirring.
Then it comes, the slow drops heavy as pigeon's eggs.
Saplings writhe, their heads wrenched up;
and the air has its earth-pollen smell.

Then the steady dumping
get-indoors-and-out-of-it downpour;
and the storm is a bore.
Trees settle to tossing and groaning,
and the cat complains from some damp place.

A sea of dark monsters squalls over our roof.
Leaves are crackling.
And, yes, on ground
the hailstones are hopping like locusts.
Short quick trajectories they bounce,
slowing like round-bodied hoppers,
to drown in browning pools.

Currawong

Currawong clans chortle
and call from steep rocks
their contempt for the wind.
In their two-word language
a whistle suggests all questions
("*Who*-is-here? *Who*-is-here?
Where's a cat? *Where's* a cat?
Go for its eyes? *Go* for its eyes?")
and *Currawong* means "I am, I did."
"Is anyone safe from the wind?"
"*Currawong.*"   "*Currawong.*"
"Brothers, is it true we hold the high places?"
"*Currawong.*"   "*Currawong.*"
"Brothers, have we killed and eaten well?"
"*Currawong.*"   "*Currawong.*"
"*Currawong.*"

Crow and Currawong Glimpses

The currawong climbs
with flickering beats,
eight frames a second.
A still on each up-beat
the live blur between,
it sculls, penguin-silent, through thick fog.

But the crow strokes hard,
each flap-wop the crack
of a parachute opening.

Cliff-edge. The crow swallow-dives.
The wind blows it back up, higher
— a piece of black plastic
the valley doesn't want.

Crow and currawong business.
Murder in the sheltered ravines.
There will be loud random flappings
postprandial chortlings
yellow eyes staring from thickets
and a scuffling mouse, or lizard, less.

Warbler

Boisterous warbler rinsing rain notes
in the light and ferny gully,
what wild love-lilt to your jenny
lures me downward from the track?
I watch your throat-pipes bulge and babble
as the gnat-choir by the tree fern,
bobbing there like lively dust-motes,
mime the *andante* of your song.
In a pause you lightly gobble
half the choir for inspiration.

Shrilly piping, loudly scratching,
terror to the grub below;
though the kite and sliding falcon
float above the valley world,
under trees and under bracken
you are all the hawk there is.
Tiny legs so thin and wiry
so pathetic in museums,
are enough for perfect landings,
every twig your balcony.

Now a fly comes booming past you,
drop your song and catch him — so!

The Giant Barrel-Gum at Mt Wilson

— has lost its top three times. The core
is a hollow hotel
of a thousand tenants.

Cautious possums take an hour
to climb its stairs; then
from an upper branch the glider leaps

to land two minutes away
in bushes of another hill.
Its surface roots flow horizontal, broad as barges.

Moss carpets the entrance-ways, rutted
where possums have clawed and skidded.
Orchids crowd on upper balconies.

The fox-brown bark
channels water down
in windless clefts.

Cockatoos nest in a broken fork,
shredding its sawdust
to the winds. No tame perch-nibblers!

And the goanna goes up the cleft,
wedging blunt claws on each side
for a handful of pigeon's eggs.

Possum litters turned
to python dung
are coiled neatly at the base.

This tree in old age
has reached the sun
though lightning-scarred.

Vertigo

The third minute on this cliff is the worst.
You throw the stone for proxy proof
of what you and gravity could do,
a furlong in five seconds.

Prudent terror trembles towards the need
that would open its breast, sweep out and soar
over warm delightful Earth. Flesh fears
to leap to the vertigo
of love, to tumble head-first
through a dozen perfect nameless flowers.
And that's the weakness in the knees,
the giddy thrill along the spine.

Katoomba Cable Car

The grey cable lines are drawn as fine
as wrinkles on a teenage brow.
In the pit of your stomach a boulder's weight
as these thin wires hold up the Car,
and your cubic foot of precious fluids.
You swing by gossamer, out on air.
The engineer smiles; his steel
is indifferent to the view.
He prods at the cable for rust,
grunts, and decides it's neither here nor there;
though your stomach swears it's from here to ever.

The Edge

The young falcon doubts her wing,
spirals up gingerly
from days in the nest
when her claws measured the air
for hold, till the heavy downed body
was out and flying.

Below her, you glimpse
a field of mud dotted with blocks
like giants' chimney pots,
and a lizard's-tail of creek
sliding off through dark-green forest
with the ochre soup of an avalanche.

You tread the gravel of hold-fasts
as softly as on the whistling air.
A grasshopper leaps
and is past you,
falling so slowly
it will have a fresh appetite
when it lands.
The steel railing nudges
below your hips' fulcrum;
you are alone on the edge,
with a million years of monkey ancestors,
watching a thistledown blow up
a hundred metres in a minute.
And your heart cries that you could fly.

Clinging

To cling, by a breaking fingernail, to an undercut cliff,
not letting your leg pivot and swing out over the valley,
and to note with one eye as you fight off panic,
the faint line of a cycad fossil in that jut of rock
by which your life will hang — this will make your hand
move about the rock, exploring, caressing,
in search of some slight peculiar thing
by which love's fingernail could cling.

Wentworth Falls

The wet ledge in the changing wind
steers away an errant
slow water-veil of white
to the forest below.

The drops whirl out,
bees leaving a hive on forage.
Or caught in the updraught they mill
with the smoky anger of a swarm.

Then climb like silver fireflies
till a long lazy sine-curve sorts them
away and down to the valley

— pearls against sky,
processioning down,
to turn invisible in the shade,
and batter the shrubs with cold hard jolts.

Wentworth Falls at Evening

Droplets in the late sun,
a shower of silver coin
into the dark valley.

Tracer bullets,
they pinpoint the breeze
in a burst of sparkles

or are pulled out like streamers
curving to forces
that hold the planets in orbit.

Going on, going out, and falling forever.
A mere chalice-full
out of that vast blessing which pours
down the Ganges, the Rhône, the Rio Negro.

And all day, every day,
these silver globules pour
into the valley where no one watches.
Men have leapt from these heights
to oblivion, wrapped
in irrelevant words of cities.

Falling Pearls Cliff

Pearls of soft fluid in zero-G
contained in a skin of self-attraction,
whirl on the upwinds of valley heat
and cliff-top bluster, floating out
to rain on the valley below.

They bunch with the mind of a shoal,
till wind pulls out their long procession
a furling scarf of outward water.
Its strands divide, until one part
— the new one — extends
a long streamer of self,
and the other breaks short,
blowing upward, back,
and is lost in mist.

Thick sunshowers wobble
and water the ledges, making
frog-lands of sunny perpetual rain.
Far below on the flat
no place or time is predictable,
yet each bush gets its turn.

Fifty metres beyond, the heath is dry.

Deep Pass Gorge

No-name Creek turns under a curl of sandstone,
and is gone with a tail-flick of silvery bubbles,
shooting down runnels carved like ancient roots,
leaping from ledges to rock-holes below.
The first hole is like Tarzan's jungle pool,
where Maureen O'Sullivan swam with a stuffed alligator
shaken by Special Effects
and the public loved it, the rare vision,
seeing their dreams in her water-hazy body
(the alligator too had his disappointments).
But the pool was real, if the ferns were potted.
Here all is real, except the dark spearman above —
him you supply from history. The fish have forgotten
and swarm to the surface in reckless shoals.

No-name Creek swirls its few litres of water an hour
under the rock's million tons.
Minnows glimmer in pools too small
for the kingfisher's wing-flash,
streams so thin the heron rests on one leg to fish.
Water spills down dark runnels, and turns
to a fall of blossom, a sift of summer snow
that lands like blessing on the ferns.
Now it leaves the sun, and dives
as if to the underworld, to planet-centre.
Its trail is a band of dark malice, until crossing a ledge
it reacts with air, a flurry of white
sifting through updraughts down.
Below, gnawing the mountain's root,
its chatter takes a keener sound. It becomes
dark solvent, gorge cutter, canyon-saw,
gutter-slicing water — that slow stone-mason
whose chisel carves round ponds.
One day the mountain of time will fall,
leaving a world of rubble
on which new streams will work.

Winter Evening

Evening seems
at first intenser blue,
fades through paleness into black.

The farmhouse in the valley
shines like a lost streetlight, cold
as a dingo's howl at midnight.

Early Dusk

Mist's eraser
rubs out the sun before day's end.
Thin-needled heaths
show green as tree-ferns.
Everywhere water invisibly
running on rock.

Parrot on Wattle

This wattle comes out of sandstone,
its lemon and green rinsed from rock and rain.
To drink it in is to know
what the black men knew:
that the blue and crimson parrot
is a primal spirit, flashing
from time to time through trees
always the same, if sometimes in pairs;
and immortal, though sometimes eaten.

Winter Dusk in a Glass Universe

The feral cat distracts, cries with love or cold.
The wind enters my tendons
turns off the warm mind
and obedient fingers.
This is a chill
not from Earth's iron core
but the cold of space
in a lonely part of the universe.
Mist snakes out of the ground,
clammy enemy of mammal blood,
stinging through wool and leather.

These cliffs, made of lake-sands, are cold, cold,
bonded by pressure and the roots of acacias.
The moon and the dreamtime have entered their being.
The stars that have gone over, ceaselessly,
and are not blotted out by the lights of men, signal
that we live in the Solar Wilderness Area,
— noses pressed to the misted glass of space, staring in
at the bright crowded city, the Milky Way,
till we all go under the ground, go under the ground for ever.

Mammals, those small hot cowards scamper out
to use hours the reptiles can't.

Forget the pluvial forests, the warm Jurassic.
At the end of all
there is only the Fire and the Cold.

"Vacant Land"

Everywhere,
red and black *Sold* boards
that doom the bush-flowers — a sign,
like dried flies on a web,
that the long-legged spinner waits nearby,
one claw upon the line.

Meanings

No myths. I would fear to insult
this delicate spiky particular land
with human meanings.

Towards Lithgow

We slow down, coming onto the plain.
A procession of sober poplars
slews from the highway to somebody's grave;
a wind prints tracks on the yellow sea of grass;
moon rolls
on the vast billiard table of the horizon,
sailing into and out from a notch in the ranges.
Out there are mouse and hunter a million fold,
and the rich seed-stores that will enter silos.

We drive into the summer,
the yellow-brown lion-skin of Australia;
drive, down barrelling lanes of speed
where the marsupial's splotch was stapled to tarmac;
driving into the harmless nights of summer,
the scratchy hay-smell, the tawny seed-awns,
and the short-sleeved nights.

Acknowledgements

The poems in this book were made possible by a 4-month Park Writers Fellowship in 1984-85, which was jointly funded by the NSW National Parks Service and by the Literary Arts Board of the Australia Council. I would like to thank the Minister and the Director of National Parks, the staff of the Literary Arts Board, all those responsible for conceiving and creating the imaginative Park Writers scheme, and those National Parks officers who shared with me their expert knowledge of the sandstone regions — in particular Bini Malcolm, Peter Mackay, Graeme Worboys, and Ian Brown. I would also like to thank John Leonard for his helpful comments on the text of these poems.

Many of the poems have been previously published in newspapers, in the annual Mattara anthologies, and in Australian or in overseas magazines (of which *London Magazine*, *Kunapipi*, *Descant* and *2PLUS2* require specific acknowledgement) or broadcast on ABC radio programs.

The Photographs

A MEGALONG BOOK

first published by
Second Back Row Press Pty Ltd 1988.
P.O. Box 43, Leura N.S.W., 2781.
Poems copyright © 1988 Mark O'Connor.
Photographs copyright © 1988 Ian Brown.
Typeset in 11/12 Plantin
by Tensor Type.
Printed in Hong Kong
by Mandarin Offset
All rights reserved.
Without limiting the rights under copyright
reserved above, no part of this publication
may be reproduced, stored in or introduced into
a retrieval system, or transmitted, in any means
(electronic, mechanical, photocopying, recording
or otherwise), without the prior written permission
of both the copyright owner and the above
publisher of this book.
National Library of Australia
Cataloguing-in-Publication data:
O'Connor, Mark, 1945-
Poetry of the Mountains.
ISBN 0 909325 57 X.
1. Blue Mountains (N.S.W.) — Poetry.
I. Brown, Ian. II. Title.
A821'.3

Design by Black Cockatoo